sinuous

For Brother Kein,

Thanks for your support and appreciation all these years!

sinuous

love,

xo

by
Lydia Kwa

Sister Lydia

TURNSTONE PRESS

sinuous
copyright © Lydia Kwa 2013

Turnstone Press
Artspace Building
206-100 Arthur Street
Winnipeg, MB
R3B 1H3 Canada
www.TurnstonePress.com

Turnstone Press gratefully acknowledges the assistance of the Canada
Council for the Arts, the Manitoba Arts Council, the Government of
Canada through the Canada Book Fund, and the Province of Manitoba
through the Book Publishing Tax Credit and the Book Publisher
Marketing Assistance Program.

Printed and bound in Canada by Friesens for Turnstone Press.

Library and Archives Canada Cataloguing in Publication

Kwa, Lydia, 1959-, author
    Sinuous / Lydia Kwa.

Poems.
ISBN 978-0-88801-447-4 (pbk.)

    I. Title.

PS8571.W3S56 2013   C811'.54   C2013-903748-9

In memory of Manuela Dias

Never abandon the sinuous path
Don't follow the direct path
Walk following the ways and roads of the old sages.

—Khmer saying from *The Cbap*

There is nothing with which it is so dangerous to take
liberties as liberty itself.

—André Breton

Preface

When I first began writing poems that would eventually make up part of this book, I came up with the working title *Road Book: Suite of Hands*, thinking of the diagrammatic books used by overland travellers to navigate across uncertain terrain—except, in this case, my road book was more a charting of tenuous, constantly shifting psychological landscape.

I created the bulk of these poems and lyrical narrative segments over a period of 14 years—from 1997 to 2011—often abandoning this project to write fiction. *sinuous* winds through the 20th into the 21st century, mapping various internal territories—my first years in Canada; a collection of dreams; visits to Japan and Singapore; reflections on trauma based on my experiences as a psychologist; the practice of ki aikido; and a range of thoughts and feelings about living in Vancouver since 1992.

As I write this preface, I am mindful that it will soon be the 10th anniversary of 9/11, as well as the death of Manuela Dias, then-managing editor of Turnstone Press, who died just days before 9/11. She was very much in my thoughts as I worked on this manuscript over the years, hence the dedication at the beginning of this book.

sinuous has been my companion for such a long time—it has been both refuge as well as a platform for arguing with myself and others as humankind continues to create beauty and wreak destruction on this precious planet. I offer *sinuous* as a gift to you, dear reader. May *sinuous* encourage you to exercise your liberty to be free.

—Lydia Kwa
August 2011

sinuous

wandering phantom

21-year-old tropical body squeezed
into Lee overalls and maroon suede Puma sneakers
whispering *lost* on a 17-hour disconnecting
connecting flight
Singapore—Manila—Honolulu—Toronto—

first ever snowflake falls on my pimpled face
on St. George Street
pre-Remembrance Day
as I trudge off to a psychoanalysis elective
at Victoria College

November 1980, Trudeau
championing bilingualism on Parliament Hill
a distant concept
for a foreign student at U of T

who sleeps on the parquet floor
of a Cabbagetown apartment
with 3 other young Chinese women

our mattresses side-by-side
compensate for
lonesome urges

Psychology 100 classes in
hallowed womb of Convocation Hall
Professor Gilmore's Beatles worship
"Here Comes the Sun"
and a new haiku before every class

if there's nothing else you remember
remember this: it all depends

in Rat School, I escape working with rats
but elect to read *The Interpretation of Dreams*
and psychoanalyze Dostoevsky's *Notes from Underground*

ᘔ

for 3 years, I live on $230 a month—rent included—
subsisting on muffins and drip coffee
salt and vinegar chips
fried rice noodles with fish cakes and bean sprouts

I study long hours, nap a lot—
fall asleep on social psychology textbooks
while bells of the Soldiers' Tower
chime for dead soldiers of two World Wars

Robarts Library has comfy anterooms in their washrooms
Laidlaw Library at University College, wide desks
for cross-arm naps
but my favourite: dusty corner at Hart House
with plush red leather sofas next to
mouldy volumes of CanLit

I detect echoes—
Hannah Arendt's notion of the banality of evil
Torok and Abraham's work on trauma and war neuroses

in a half-asleep daze
I stumble along Philosopher's Walk,
cut across campus, past Queen's Park
through the Annex, Yorkville, Bloor and Yonge streets

Toronto's chill eats into my bones
disenfranchised no longer a concept
the once-unquestioned privilege of growing up
Chinese in Singapore
replaced by minority status on a student visa
displaced Hokkien speaker in the Cantonese milieu of
Spadina

I don't understand this idea they call *multiculturalism*

the person I'd been before Canada
seems hollow
or too muffled by layers of wool and snow
now identified by negation:
non-citizen
non-white

nothing seems to reflect me these days

keep trying to peer through the windows
of other people's houses
unsure what I'm looking for

unmoored from the shell of
my previous life

secrets left behind
I can't speak of

but still—

inside my body that uneasy
phantom lives

ᘒ

days spent wandering
while nights are dedicated to
falling
into dreams
under
ground

I am without hands. The arms are there, familiar, easy, so that some part of my routine intelligence insists on the truth of hands. My eyes see their shadowy outline, but they exist only as phantoms without the will to search for occupation.

While wandering through the first dream, grief creeps into me, one memory stretching into another. Tenderness a fleeting pulse from the centre of my chest. I glance at a small dark table in the far corner, glass bowl choked with apricots, their skins fresh and waiting.

The sight of vulnerability.

But I don't believe in my own touching, *I whisper at the ash-grey walls, suspecting someone might hear me. Someone I could bruise with my hands, if I still had them. Someone walking around in a different dream suite, whose own mind has erased some other aspect of the body's original freedom.*

I imagine each body I have stroked and rejected, until the memories ache at my wrists.

൭

phantom, adj.	hand, n.
illusive *spectral*	*a worker* *influence*

phantom, n.	hand, v.t.
a deceitful appearance *an immaterial form*	*manipulate* *transfer*

൭

ghostly hands
psychic shadows

speak through feeling
crushed, and going against

       webbed fingers want to unfurl
       at the edge of tangible

a memory of father's hands
beating against my heart

       attuned to rhythms of fear
       gripped by childhood tremors

a memory of mother's hands
habitual

phantom kernel
hides within
also an occasional
escape artist
floats willy-nilly
or zig-zags
underground

while wandering
alien landscape
discovers
colonial imprints
submerged memory

pulse of
discontent rankles
yet inexpressible
beneath enforced smile

awaiting

return of the child
who cried
whose hands curled in

What I read in a book picked off the shelf of a bookstore.
The quote enters now through the deeper door of sleep,
and stands solitary in the shadows of the next room.

It was a man who wrote about the primacy of Desire, the
spontaneous gesture of Need. Distinguishing between
raised arms impelled by desire, and the body's open arc of
need.

In the corner of dark mahogany panels, I squat as if waiting
for a train. To listen better to the woman pacing the floor
above. That creaking presence, anxiety seeping through
rhythm. Until the beat of that other's life throbs in my mind,
heavy and measured.

Nothing thinks as clearly as the body. I raise my arms to
the ceiling, trying to reach the woman who paces. How
can I bruise her with this truth, past the boundaries of her
guarded life?

Light and air, long before any reason to forget the beauty of
apricots. In a different dream, the woman above me exists
in the same room, squatting next to me.

I am still, sense the impending journey from the feet up.

ɞ

crossing the continent from east coast to west
leaving snow and ice for mountains and forest

lonely in dystopian un-paradise
until mythology enters stage right—
            love of one's life

endorphin rush of
unity/unification/unison
romance of
she echoing me echoing her

in the beginning *she* lived in the same room
but then, but then   *(stutter, words adrift)*
she was expelled, or was it me?

longstanding desire to reel in
the unreachable woman

she who wept from across the lake
while I, deep in dream
fished for land

do her eyes travel
inward bound
            where *she* hurts

matter material mater
knew her
before I met her—

The red room. Large and echoing. Without the pretence of painting or photographs. Frames left hanging after theft.

I look out of a window, and in the distance at the edge of the world, a vision. It travels toward me slow as a breath exhaled. I walk out of the room onto the dusty streets. A walled city, yellow bricks carrying sunlight in their pores, a hundred feet high.

I will send her a letter. *Reconciling myself to this sojourn. Thirty more paces, I arrive at the edge of a courtyard. Warriors, all men, in sea-green breastplated armour. Their arms trace circles through the air.*

I recognize the moves, the muscled art. I turn to address the feminine man, I am familiar with this but it is the ornamentation of temples I am more interested in.

Behind the warriors, a low temple roof. Paler than the breastplates, a faint turquoise border of ceramic reliefs, curls and waves, ancient secret.

&

dreaming fantastical
dreaming fiction
to sleep in
another bed
some time in the future past

&

uncurl stiff
imperfect frond
deadened night

flying fish
triple eyed

departed
species othered

anonymous ones
buried under debris
twinned towers
of desire and violence

but still
memory struggle wants
recovery of lost syllables

who and what
fingers and fins and frogs

poisoned
mutating

can I hear?
is it possible
they call out?

collapsing ache
of stranger and
stranger

gods and goddesses of my dreaming
wandering away from my grasp

she's gone
they're gone

memory of *them* leaks through the interstices

does a dream pose a question
or is it memory in disguise?

is it a taint from daylight ego
or a truth?

wish to wake up happy
but rattled by a persistent wail in the world
no amount of sleep
can stifle

lotusland pain drifts
separated from the body of
content sighs
phantom pain
left to wander the open alleys

a beggar sleeps
next to the burnt shell
of Ho Tak Kee
below a mural about Love
rain soaks the prone figure
through to the core

The rats float up from invisible to visible in this light-filled room tinged with oceanic greens and blues. The creatures are indestructible, eluding my grasping hands. My companion is able to pluck them out of their magical appearing, walks to the window to drop them over the edge. They never hit the ground. She repeats this act countless times but the rats keep returning.

Mr. Architect shows me the plan of the house. Look here, *he says, pointing to the quilted fabric.* This is the core. You've tried to defend yourself by sealing off your centre, but it's not working. *He points to the border of blue around the pink.* Rats penetrate you because they're coming up from the foundation.

Pre-dawn, 4 am, when I can sense the transitional gasp already begin, from dormant hiding to waking camouflage. Thick vermillion curtains shield me as I lie in bed listening to the call of chickadees sheltering in the hawthorn tree. So compelling this summons that I rise from the bed and pull the curtains back.

not raining rats outside
not even men in bowler hats
not Magritte's poke at deception
not even the lost city of Golconda

everything begins and ends in the basement
unseen, taken for granted

root consciousness
from which all seeds grow

where the architect of knowing lives

does the hand remember
its first
reach
for
breast's rich
satiation

mouth's confession
sucking trust

inevitable
entanglement
the tilt
of desire
?

House stripped down to its bare girders. I'm a drifter shocked at devastation, lost in my own home. Instead, the harsh openness of nature, moist ground matted with dead leaves.

Must prove myself to a homeless man, that this piece of ground was once my living room floor.

He accepts my story and lets me lie down.

what remains intrinsic
when home is stripped of
privilege?

ego pleads her case
with a drifter who holds no pretensions
about territoriality—

he simply accepts because
there is no such thing as
mine versus *yours*

Christ the magic saviour
lived by the sea

neither Peter's nor Paul's
but still, voice of a peacemaker
prophet who wails his Jesus Puff tune
near Waterfront Station

heart—

    thump sound
    garbled
    in the mouths of spin
    doctors

kisses vaporize
in damp dirt alleys
behind vacated storefronts

beggars for mercy
in the glare of campaigns
sleek concrete and glass

must dive into garbage dumpsters
for possibilities

social housing social housing social housing
a mantra that competes with reams
of development plans awaiting approval at city hall

&

*Standing naked while the woman—somewhat terrified and
aware of her weakness—languishes, victim on the bed.
He brags about knowing how to conquer. Tweaks his right
nipple, and in place of his flaccid penis, a long hand shoots
out between his legs.*

*Mostly reminiscent of a human being's, yet the pale,
translucent skin betrays some shades of red and black veins
along the webs between fingers. Beckoning from a sunken
world.*

&

Atlantean truths
soaked in amniotic embryonic
textures

unvoiced
underworld

unspoken

*If you insist, I will tell you: "My mother is dead." They tell
me that it is so all day long, and I simply agree with them to
get them off my back.*

*...I love my mother, I adore her, have never left her. If she
were dead, I would despair, I would feel very sad, would
feel abandoned and alone. Well, I don't feel anything; I am
not sad at all, I don't cry; thus, she is not dead.*

Irène assumed bizarre postures
in the hospital ward
at Salpêtrière

stared at an empty bed
brought a glass to the lips
of her imaginary mother
still in the throes of suffering

open your mouth, drink, answer me

hands fussed
four eternal hours
arranging
the body in bed
until a convulsion and sleep
lent temporary reprieve

days and nights in limbo
in Ergriffenheit—

she is not dead

      memory that will not arrive
      not yet knowing able to know

she, the living
seized by the dead
laughed through the funeral

ԑ҇

      (unvoiced memory fragment
      set adrift, lapped at the edge of

ԑ҇

It is only for convenience that we speak of it as a "traumatic memory." The subject is often incapable of making the necessary narrative which we call memory regarding the event; and yet (s)he remains confronted by a different situation in which (s)he has not been able to play a satisfactory part, one to which (her) adaptation had been imperfect, so that (s)he continues to make efforts at adaptation.

                    —Pierre Janet

how of forget
what of remember

rough, honest stutter

stranger at the door
shadowy intimation
keeps returning
insistent knocks
loud louder yet disavowed

curious about
sunken truths

how the mind works
how healing occurs

I turn from textbook theories
toward listening to strangers in my office
their mute underworlds
articulating
through speech and body

how to bridge
the rift of suffering?
some gesture, however slight
to diminish that sense of
all alone, no one knows

heinous tortures
accounts of heartless betrayals
garden variety strains of cruelty

one thousand and one nights
ceases to be a romantic notion
when these rampant tales of suffering
keep me awake
wondering
what else is beneath
frantic despair

   they have come to this country
   seeking asylum

how to recover
the lost suffering lonely hopeless
from out of the

       wound *as in* clockwork
       wound *as in* mark

skin peeled with whips
bodies strapped
lowered into water, electrocuted

fed rat-infested food
starved raped burned

poisoned with promises
of harm to their loved ones

muscles bones blood
in sustained state of overwhelm
neural signals firing
extreme threat

pushed to feral
brink

picture a city razed, smouldering still
unending search for survivors, buried

likewise
the devastation of a tormented mind
buried embers survive
amid ruins and shards

unspoken meanings
lodged beneath the
cant chant

closed limbic loop

slippery slope of denial:
can't can't can't

meanings that beckon
to the silenced in me

which part of the mind
overrides suffering?

to remain caught in sheer repetition
of traumatic experience

or discover the will
to transcend

is it merely brain tissue
prefrontal cortex
where
mindfulness resides?

what makes someone capable
of creating a new paradigm
and living it?
who owns that willingness to create
who's that so-called architect of the soul?

℔

alert and observant of others
while I suffer
rasp-edged echoes of
an unvoiced kernel

my lungs heave with sorrow

what about that dream of sojourn
in an ancient city?

I long
to receive my own love letter
from within walls imbued with
sublime light

to be softened and tamed

I feel miscast
as foot soldier
readying for war

ॐ

language that insists
on singular meaning
outfitted
for conflict
misses
a dream's escape route

ॐ

resting in the dark chamber of an early morning cab
I wrap a rosewood mala around my right wrist
red and white silken tassels
brush against my clasping left hand

at the Vancouver airport café
the South Asian cashier catches a glimpse of the mala
        is it 21 or 108 beads?

on the plane heading toward the equator
I wonder how I'd stayed alive all those years—

        while they performed true to social scripts
        written with audience participation—
        she, the perennial thorn
        he, the likable hero—

        I, sick and troubled, expressed the wound

✆

My mother's flat may overlook the ocean, but she has
stopped going for walks along the beach. *Too much of a
bother,* she replies.

I stay at a nearby hotel and visit daily.

It is December 2002. I haven't come since 1998 yet she
makes no reference to 9/11, acts as if there isn't any
evidence of it in her consciousness. Her face is blank,
revealing no emotion. At least, that I can decipher.

Chaos, heat, humidity—the pollution of the whole housing
estate undergoing upgrading—those oppressive fields of
influence crowd us as we sit across from each other, staring.
Her silence feels monumental.

The dark-skinned labourers from Sri Lanka and Burma
are each paid seventeen dollars for each day of work. My
mother gushes over their bright orange coveralls. She takes
pity on them, offers them packets of vacuum-sealed fruit
juices at 5 pm as they leave her flat at the end of their work
day.

Alone with me, she falls silent. Then she begins her cleaning
ritual, wipes the edges of the iron grille framing the kitchen
window. Her body swings like a pendulum left right left
right, her hands frantic. Words explode out of her, raging
against contamination: the dirt, chipped tiles, dusty plaster.

She asks me five times in a row, *can you still see that mark on the floor?*

She is furious. Perfection never arrives.

...*a history that literally has no place, neither in the past, in which it was not fully experienced, nor in the present, in which its precise images and enactments are not fully understood.*

—Cathy Carruth

my mother doesn't speak about the Japanese Occupation
except to say that as a young girl
she lined up with servants
for bags of rice

       her generation of silence
       must rattle inside me
       forbidding disclosures

       my psyche has to do double time
       for what she wouldn't reveal

in the 1960s my mother's mother was straitjacketed
and sedated many times at Woodbridge Hospital

my uncle too, an occasional patient there

for years I feared I would go insane
some genetic curse

Mom still speaks incessantly
about how others fail her
        my uncle cheated her of inheritance money
        my father spent too much

her tone is jarring, frenetic

                      (betrayed abandoned misunderstood

I urge myself, *listen deeper*

she isn't dead so why do I cry
assume bizarre postures
to conceal the deaths hidden in living?

100 years separate Pierre Janet's Irène and me

I mourn the mother who has disappeared
a shell in her place
her spirit ejected by the unspoken

ↁ

red lights and hot neon promises
emblazon Hotel 81's façade
yet my tiny room is cold, devoid of glamour

late at night
ruckus of hookers in the corridor

scent of their furtive work
distracting

how to meditate
while feeling futile?

heat seething in my chest

His Holiness the Dalai Lama's words
your greatest enemy is your greatest teacher

potent medicine choked
in my unforgiving heart

I open the window to
blast of humid air

stare across the vacant lot
riddled with
gargantuan glyphs of concrete

sentinels as immovable as dogma

～

sharp light next morning
pierces gauze curtains
followed by a soft knock at the door

the housekeeper needs to clean my room
spies my mala on the side table
confides that her friends think her backward
because she hasn't converted to Christianity

surprised that with my education
I've gone the other direction

        I recall the contempt I was taught
        for anything non-Jesus

        progress simply included
        a colonizing God

outside the hotel, waiting for a taxi
noonday sun scorching hot

no room for subtle shadows here
nowhere to dwell safely without scrutiny

I yearn for release from snares of the literal
stretched skin of living

I am leaving again
this time for somewhere unfamiliar

sojourn

The trains to Nara from Nagoya are the first I take in this
country. I speak no Japanese but read enough Kanji to
find my way. Winter cold cuts deeply into the body. Low
buildings huddled together, landscape drenched in dream.
Everyone assumes I'm Japanese until I open my mouth.
Kembutsu-nin. A flicker of realization in their eyes, *spectator
and tourist after all.*

ornate manhole covers
adorn the humble streets of Nara

nothing left mundane
nothing ordinary

narrow alleys tight with habitation
twisted paths, sudden treasures, dead ends

shiver of December damp
as I head away from the centre of town
trudge up the slope to Todaiji
against the gentle slant of rain veiling

strangers wandering through
green expanse of Nara koen
where chestnut-brown deer
          bright eyed and fearless
mingle with humans

shelter under
soaked paper prayers

knotted 'round pine branches overhead
        swarms of white whispered needs
        beside the stream

nothing left ordinary
nothing simple

I join the crowd of pilgrims
enter the dimmed hall
of Daibutsuden
encounter the enormity of a bronze Buddha
caressed by swirls of incense smoke

I skirt around the solid presence
aware there is nothing
to possess
                what exactly am I looking for?

presumably conducting background research
for *The Walking Boy*
searching for evidence of 8th-century
Buddhist art and architecture

I scribble notes
in a spiral-bound notebook
with yellow water-proofed cover
        just a touch of sun
        for the shadow in me

much later
spend the afternoon at a nearby café
thawing with hot kohii

stunned by the sexy spread
nude alpha male
supine in French *Vogue*
coolly sipping his cup of coffee
       keeping me company
       in my favourite fantasy of
       alone together

never mind that I have no idea
what this journey is all about

I resume wandering through the maze of alleys
surprised I've finally made it to Japan

in 1970 my father went to Osaka for Expo
part of a choir singing at the Singapore pavilion
but my mother had refused to go

was it because of unvoiced hatred—
of what the Japanese military had done
in Manchuria and Nanjing?
or was it because of her own experiences
during the Japanese Occupation of Singapore?

               I will never know

trust instead my instincts
to negotiate a path around such unknowns

plastic stand-ins for food
in a restaurant window
trigger hunger pangs

variations on the theme of unagi
      cool slivers next to crunchy tsukemono
      grilled and laid on top of fragrant gohan
      or steaming hot in soup

600, 700, 1300 yen
and up

thunderstorm rages
bullies bamboo screens

I look up at
a wild and brooding sky
then rush in
      collapsing my wet umbrella
      under the flapping noren

the next day I take a small bus out of the city

stretches of farmland
dotted with occasional houses

countryside spacious for the eyes
Lonely Planet guidebook on my lap

at the entrance to Horyuji Temple
I'm met by Kuniko the tour guide
who summons her two friends
Keiko and Kiyoko

ancient bronze body of Yumechigai-Kannon
Avalokiteshvara for good dreams
stands on a lotus throne
in the treasure hall

      left hand holding vase of nectar at her side
      right hand raised to bestow refuge

the three K's
trill in delicate canary-chorus
delighted to share
that She protects us in our dreaming

we gaze upon
her peaceful visage
the glass no barrier
to our yearnings

        she is Mother
        waking dream

        salve
        for the restless
        tormented mind

ℒ

leaving Nara on the slow train

enter Kyoto's modern JR station
of cold, grey stone with glass heights

bus 205…stop at Kawaramachi-Shomen…
cross the road and walk about two minutes

reach Ryokan Yuhara, the Japanese inn
on Kiyamachi next to the old canal
cherry trees along Takase River

the river that used to link travellers
between Tokyo and Osaka

I remove my shoes at the entrance
of the ryokan
select a pair of house slippers

upstairs, just next to the staircase
is my room with a wooden plaque *Mount Hiei*

      recalling the famous mountain
      off limits to women for much of Japanese history
      once a site for gods and demons
      marathon monks

well, now——Hiei has been breached
if only temporarily

a rustic tatami room
futon tidily rolled up
extra space heater

no sight or sound of other guests
a quiet sojourn, indeed

at dusk
out on the street
walk past the small café
serving mostly oden
stewing saltily for hours

I'm nervous entering the sento—
how does it all work?
lockers for clothes, pay for towel
I hear male voices in the adjoining baths
as I enter the women's room

wash at the taps, sitting on a stool
keep company with other naked women

no self-consciousness detectable
in this most ordinary
and unpretentious baring

I dip my cleansed body into a dark delicious stew
of fragrant herbs

return to a simple, pure pleasure
let the ease soak through

falling asleep fast in *Hiei*
but startled awake at 5 am
hands reach to grasp
emptiness

imaginary woman
eluding
my embrace

she whose breast
I yearn to consume

the way I'm consumed by absence

        if mind is mirror
        who else could she be?

I worry about my nose
growing to demon length
eyes bulging with delusion

anxiety propels me
out the door

early morning at Nishiki Market
chock-full of desirables

empty mouth
searching for

tofu trembling sexy
in a steaming wooden vat

pickles crinkled kinky
in coy taster bowls

transient fragrance
from large canisters of tea

flashy tentacles of marinated octopus
tempting proposition

miniature, rotund eggplants
gleam in vinegared juices

grades of bonito
paper thin
swell the bins

in early afternoon light, wandering through Gion
before the geisha and maiko are awake

I delight in stores dedicated
to a single commodity
        one hundred varieties of umeboshi
        fifty kinds of incense
        twenty types of desserts made with arrowroot
        served alongside frothing, neon-green matcha

while sucking sweet arrowroot noodles
between my lips
I fantasize Haruki Murakami
entering the café and sitting with me
to discuss *The Wind-Up Bird Chronicle*

of course, we sip matcha together

I will ask, *how did you find the courage*
to stare down that warring darkness
write past the horrific torture scene?

I need his encouragement
to write against fear—
somehow it matters that he's exactly 10 years older
an only child like me
and partial to jazz

if the inner route is to be arduous
could it at least be buffeted by the pleasure
of a sublime encounter?

The pleasure that comes from pleasurable surroundings is
       not true pleasure.
   Only with the pleasure obtained in the midst of
       suffering
   Can one see the true movements of the mind.

                                        —Hung Ying-ming

At the Kyoto Museum of Contemporary Art. My first
encounter with Nobuyoshi Araki's photos, *Hana Jinsei:
Human Life in Bloom.*

Grid of Polaroids inhabits a wall, constellation of extinction
and arousal confounded. Desired women exposed, kimonos
loosened and no longer concealing. Bodies trussed up and
readied, juxtaposed with shots of dead flowers.

To stare at an overblown red tulip is to be disturbed by the
heart of its dying. Tears rise to my eyes when I realize these
images don't exist separate from me.

Is it just me, or are you into it too?

is a person who is bound
the obvious victim?

question of advantage or dis—
vantage is critical

leaving the war behind
or taking it with us

inside the bound
a hidden code
for what torments us still

pain of generations elides
into arousal

distills to a symbol
of breasts and sex
enclaved in the imagination

rope was a holy thing once
used to bind sacred objects
during the Jomon period

pottery shaped by the imprints
of rope on wet clay

from evidence of the earliest civilization
to marks of modern brutality—
what journey in the minds of men
did this rope take
to be transformed from sacred to defiled?

to become an instrument of torture—
to contort bodies into aching restriction

hence, the erotic danger—
a shadow zone between worship and degradation

how does an object acquire such mythical power?

blame it on rope man woman beast saviour
        objects swept up
        by the churnings of our desire

pure or profane
an act of the mind

thirty-three bays of Sanjusangendo
display 1001 wooden statues of Kannon

all those arms those hands!

                had I not dreamt?

                        the polymorphous
                        ornamentation of temples

why surprised
at the insistent plea for
mercy?

why deny
we need profound rescue
for what ails us?

33 the atomic number of arsenic
poison except in trace amounts—
Arsenicum Album homeopathic remedy
for great anguish and restlessness

Triangulum in the northern sky
Messier 33 Galaxy
path of the sun embracing Summer Solstice

33 vertebrae
in the human spine from the coccyx up

is the Divine separate from us?
or a presence that permeates
the ground of our being?

Kannon, hear our cries
sense this dire need
to transcend alienation

sinuous

Tracking the known path down Commercial, wanting to find newness. Trying to look past lazy seeing. It's an illusion, this notion of familiarity. Nothing has stayed the same. The heterosexual couples are different every week-end, migrating from Kitsilano for a cheap, fun meal at the Latin Quarter and dancing cheek-to-cheek.

Late at night, competing with salsa rhythms, insistent blaring from a ghetto blaster in front of Alpha Video across the street, Diana Ross's voice, disembodied but powerful nonetheless, *My world is empty without you, babe.*

feeling besieged after
too many days of rain

sunshine today
seems out of place

I drag myself out of the apartment
a lacklustre stride

    a man crosses the street ahead
    steady, determined

I follow him for three blocks
to the Britannia mat room

    character for "energy"
    hung in the centre of the padded front wall

the word *qi* in Chinese
pronounced *ki* in Japanese

another sign in the right hand corner of the dojo:

Principles of Mind Body Coordination

Think of your one point
Completely relax
Have a light posture
Extend your mind

déjà vu, this was the dojo
where I tried to practise
ki aikido 12 years prior

quit classes
when fear of getting hurt
overwhelmed me

I had put it all behind me—
or so I thought—

now, I want to leave
language in the background
bow to a different path

how to find the one point—
4 fingers below the navel
then contract the belly
and feel it deep inside
still relaxed

stand lightly
on the balls of the feet
without rocking back on the heels

corner step
      make it bigger
      bigger

let the legs be moved
from the one point

      you're asking me to trust
      that power comes
      from the hips?

yes, let the heart be moved
by the hips

think of your one point—

      descend
      from intellectual cut-off
      to the elixir field
      where a buddha waits
      to be born

completely relax—

      startling injunction
      not to blame the external
      but make medicine
      for one's own misery

have a light posture—

> how tight
> my body is with the tension
> of rumination!

extend your mind—

> so—if mind exists
> beyond the body's parameters—
> dismantle my preconceptions,
> why don't I?

renegades
drawn by gravity
of need

as if we're exiles from the land of cool
and must find refuge here

trace our inheritance to Morihei Usehiba
early photos
the warrior's fierce look
firm jaw

late photos,
old man
with soft, penetrating eyes
wispy beard

what drained the war from him?
whether to believe the story
that he was transformed
by a kami when he went to the well for water

      YouTube videos of him
      throwing off young men
      as if they were mere insects

      or wielding the jo with
      miraculous speed

      spirit flash of dragon
      glimpsed between movements

          then there's us—
          motley crew of O-Sensei's heirs

gutter realities—
        smell fear close up
        breath's threat
        rush of
        skin muscle hair sweat

        hands grab
        arms resist
        touch, a bomb
        exploding in the gut

fighting mind
fraught
with old texts:
retaliate subjugate erase

if not predator, then prey

blueprint of destruction
revealed in the hands

cellular memory

I watch my sensei, think
father, brother, son
I never had

not punished for being flawed
not rejected for making mistakes

encouraged to
show up on the mat
keep practising

patience is homeopathic
       seeps slowly
       into my nervous system

surrender
blend
harmonize

takes a long time
to make deep shifts

yet my inner resolve grows
with each repetition of a move

what began as a distant concept
slowly becomes wordless knowing

this curative practice:
be willing to fail
a thousand times ten
and notice failure
in order to learn

        I need this kind of
        physical engagement

        face to face
        with my own fears

        agitating that space
        between me and the other

                materializes
                the phantom, unvoiced yet

                wandering the circuits
                of familiar alienation
                uneasy, not quite
                ready for peace

Your mind should be in harmony with the functioning of the universe; your body should be in tune with the movement of the universe; body and mind should be bound as one, unified with the activity of the universe.

—Morihei Ueshiba

standing between
heaven and earth
yet forgetting how divine

how to divine
this vertex where I inhabit
a point of intervention
in constant flux

Tao breeds the One
One creates Two, then
Three, unfolding myriad realities

so too, the Three returning
ultimately to One

a sinuous curve uniting
body with mind
dissolving the rift between
me and my enemies

feelings in my body unfamiliar
charged with some odd capacity
strength yet not muscle
invisible to the eyes
yet sensed
smaller than small
bigger than biggest
grows
ebbs
billows beyond

the strong man laughs and exclaims
I love it when you throw me right

oh yeah I love it too, honey
even though your hairy arms
remind me of my father

don't take it personally, okay?

(are you here to help me practise my defensive moves
or is there some agenda in your attack
you have yet to settle
within yourself?

why should I trust you?
I never know
if you will love
or betray

(so glad we're not married

counting weapons is like counting votes
it depends on who's counting

—Julian Berger

Also depends on how one counts.

Whether attention alights on the moment of truth, where
body confesses the mind's tension. Or whether the habit is
to forget the presence of habit itself.

Count the number of times hands feel the grip of weapons,
wanting to eliminate the enemy.

Or count remembering any moment when peace prevailed.

66

Same people different each time. A pun of permutations.
One moment, dangerous. Another, offering friendship.

Practising to learn, practising how to keep safe and not
harm. The binary folds into each encounter, and dissolves.
Unfolds, and curves away from straight or forward.

in a moment of panic
I force my wrist
out of a hold

pain
doubles me over

The mind of attachment arises from the stopping mind. So does the cycle of transmigration. This stopping becomes the bonds of life and death.

—Takuan Soho

Vulnerable at the loss. Left hand swells, temporarily disabled. I google wrist: 8 carpal bones linked by intrinsic ligaments, crossed by extrinsic web of interconnections.

Recalling the vision of wandering through that dream suite where I lost the power of my hands.

Hadn't believed in my own touching. Didn't know the truth of hands. Does it take a loss to return me to myself?

A dream materializes, aching at my wrist.

how can you succeed if you don't learn?
how can you learn if you don't fail?
how can you succeed if you don't fail?

        fear is my injury
        injury, my learning

reconcile with the pain
one gradual gesture at a time
one limit stretched
one sliver of habit
dislodged

I feel despair and desperation
cascade of panic

I crave
light that warms
heat that illuminates
the spaces between

I practise *ki* breathing
in my apartment
while others engage on the mat

an inner voice pronounces—
loneliness is not a natural consequence
of being alone

feels as if I've been conducting an ongoing
field study over several lifetimes

every breath
a deliberate choice

clearing first with
guttural *haaaa*

then draw in air
to fill the lungs
imagine energy sent through the body
down to the toes

up and down that spine of necessity

practice to usurp
my nasty habit of ruminating

enter body and mind
fully into each breath

the act of breathing
as a form of unconditional regard—
going out then returning
without hesitation

I stare out the window
to the park across the street
children on the swings

am I willing to protect
the vulnerable?

allow the faces of children
to become beloved

that word: *allow*

as if closing the gap
returning two to one

that child, that attacker
that past, that present

that phantom, kernel

now
harmonized

and so—
remain open to love
        fingers of ocean touching shore

after six weeks I return
my feet grateful for the dirty dojo mat

wrist bound in tape
nerves still raw

hard to describe what's changed
except to say that
the urge to fight fear with fear
has drastically diminished
want instead to stay peaceful
within

stay stay stay

that voice again

instead of flights into
fantasies or bad memories

I must beckon and soothe
like a parent coaxing
a frightened child
back from her nightmare

True Victory is Self-Victory

—Morihei Ueshiba

if I could be so fortunate as to meet the kami
who will inspire me
to move
like water freed from a well
ungraspable

back to original freedom

the body thinking clearly

I anticipate a time
when I can fully enter the land of the living

phantom returned home

sinuous
stream overturning
stone wound

base

base, n.
that on which a thing stands
or, as in chemistry, a substance
that reacts with an acid to form
a salt, or dissolves in water
to form hydroxyl ions

Gatecrashers are not welcome
—*National Post,* July 22,1999

Ship's passengers must be sent home
—*The Vancouver Sun,* July 23, 1999

Boat people who need a return ride
—*The Globe and Mail,* July 23,1999

large boats arrive on the shores of a foreign land
        mythic echoes of conquest

glaring, flagrant hostility toward
vessels that spill human contents
        past boundaries and borders

a spill that challenges presumptions
of place:

> *it is not your place to speak*
> *out of turn*
> *hard to place that face*

do you honestly
mean *mi casa su casa?*

> *Coming to this faraway land, Canada,*
> *My hope is fulfilled.*
> *Why do you treat me like this,*
> *Do you think this is justice?*
> *I wait and wait and*
> *Don't know when you'll release me.*
> *Days passed, months passed,*
> *How could I not be sad?*
> *May I ask what the Immigration Board*
>   *and the Judge*
> *Really want to do with me?*

Sung by female Fujian boat migrants incarcerated
at Burnaby Correctional Centre for Women

Admiral Zheng He a eunuch
arrived on our shores
in the 13th century
long before the Europeans

      exception to the rule
      that male genitals are necessary
      for success

(I think about my ancestors
                  arriving in junks
                  on the shores of Sumatra and Singapore

"Orient" being a romantic notion
fenced-in stage
where the whole East is corralled

Together for an hour on Saturday mornings in the chilly
visiting room of the Burnaby Correctional Centre for Women.
Buzzed in by guards, us from the outside, the Fujian women
from the locked quarters upstairs.

Her body quakes.

The tremor of her chilled hands as they clutch mine, quiver of her lips as she pleads for help. Shadow self, Mermaid stripped of sea legs, imprisoned for almost twenty months, all because she's one of 599 who dared to arrive on boats from Fujian province. The day after she's released from prison, stories of the violence she experienced in China spill from her.

Reverberations unsettle the air between us.

in over a decade since the arrival of the boats
a handful of migrants obtain
legitimate status
the rest, gone underground
working in restaurants in New York
or back to the Mainland

tolerate, v.t.
to allow, without prohibiting
to permit
to recognize and respect
to put up with/endure
as in: medicine, to have tolerance for
(substance/pathogen)

*The visions of men are widened by travel and contacts with
citizens of a free country will infuse a spirit of independence
and foster yearnings for freedom in the minds of the
emasculated subjects of alien rule.*

—Gurdit Singh Sandhu

this country I adopted
has bred a dark history of hatred:
      1885 Chinese Head Tax and 1923 Exclusion Act
      racial segregation in schools
      theft of aboriginal lands
      residential school abuse
      internment of Japanese Canadians
      the *Komagata Maru* incident in 1914
      detention of Tamil migrants

so much more…

illusory peacemaking *kanata*
where polite citizens
welcome asylum seekers
with ambivalent embrace

tolerate sadly cheapened
cliché a sleek poseur

here I am in west coast paradise lost
burnished Gold Mountain

*…pseudologia phantastica, that form of hysteria which is
characterized by a peculiar talent for believing one's own
lies…the essence of hysteria is a systematic dissociation,
a loosening of the opposites which normally are held
together. It may even go to the length of a splitting of the
personality, a condition in which quite literally one hand no
longer knows what the other is doing.*

—Carl Jung

Race represented as theory. Theory presented as if a unitary
truth.

There's a lie that stability means unchanging nature.
Archetypes frozen within fixed parameters. What we
worship, on the altars of our minds.

Ergreifer—one who seizes

grip of stereotype
archetype of seizure
fugue of the patriarch
patronage of the seized

rising tide of asylum seekers on our planet
                    flux movement shift
                    flee torture strife war starvation

aching need for sanctuary

in the news on 11.11.10—

war veterans homeless

gamma ray bubbles
in the Milky Way

speculation that ex-premier Campbell
will be remembered favourably

forecast for the next hundred years:
more war
more plague
more calamity

what was Old Testament
news again

After the long wait, my father receives his heart transplant.
The surgeon is a hard man to pin down. Even the fleeting
image of his white coat an unsure thing, as I search through
various rooms in the hospital, devoid of the usual antiseptic
smells. Instead, there are hints of balmy breezes outside
the open windows, this kampong house of teak, creaking
floorboards on which my bare feet pace.

The surgeon, when I find him, is not as frightening as my
projection. Your turn will come soon, *he reassures me,* a
new heart, very different than your father's.

heir, n.
one who succeeds
to property or position
inherits qualities, social position
or the past

needed to leave the country
to dream
a new heart

shed inheritance
from inside out
when outside of in-

still, beneath my feet creaks
that rustic past

dreaming double truths
my father, me
merged into one—

only to veer again into
unspeakable taboo—
that change of heart
and all it entails

prodigal daughter
drifts away from the patriarch
disinherits herself

or perhaps not her self
but the communal will as defined by history

treason—
against the construct of Filial Piety

consider disavowing the split view called paradox

in the gap between two soapboxes
is the abyss
an opening

My guide asks me to choose my own path, and to allow my
mother to go on ahead without me. That is her direction, not
yours, he reminds me. Much later, finding myself wandering
through the dirty alleys of an unknown city, I meet the young
woman who will become my teacher. She shows me the
shell of a large building, all the rooms no longer existent.
The building waits to be demolished. She has found the right
kind of bomb. Studded with precious stones, like ornaments
adorning the body of a bodhisattva, this sphere will dismantle
all the remaining illusions of solidity.

uncommon destroyer
recovering from the earth
jewel powers

she has the feel of an angel or
bodhisattva whose gems
impart transcendence

could she rescue me from Bad Daughter syndrome?
where being away signifies failure
and failure to conform signifies disloyalty?

what does it mean to be loyal?
why is love sacrificing?
what is the meaning of sacrifice?

I diverge from my mother's path
in search of a different direction

        she feels abandoned—
        in her darkest moments I am
        that failed daughter
        never good enough
        never convincing
        with the small morsels of love I offer

to inflect that word *abandon*
with its alternate meaning
        to depart, with the intent
        of release
                    dismantle and
        demolish
        structures I inherited
        no longer inhabitable

I visit my mother in 2011
weeks before she turns 77—

she hardly speaks to me
waves me off when I try to engage

is she lucid? angry?
suffering an unknown malaise?

she manages to walk to the nearby wet market
almost every morning I'm there
returns with fresh fish even before I set out

Mom washes my clothes, cooks half the meals
no longer watches TV or reads the papers
spends long hours sitting with eyes closed or sleeping

I witness panic attacks that sheath her
in a swirl of inaccessibility

her fragility ignites
a spark of tenderness in me

her panic, my standard to bear

I desperately
want to discover what she needs—

past cruelties, neglect, misunderstandings
no longer obstacles
to my wish to uncover the deeply buried gem

my heart opens up
despite the absence of words

I weave between the blocks of flats in
Marine Parade housing estate
along sheltered walkways connecting
one block to the next

basal ganglia hubs of action selection
routine behaviours travelled in memory

here, a nucleus of habit
there, a burst of new

> *where is the core of automatic?*
> *what unfurls the delicate track of*
> *venturing?*

I head to the wet market early
air cool with pre-dawn birdcalls
before the scorch of late morning

mingle with housewives and grandmas
take in sharp fresh smells of green

commanding shouts of sellers bounce off
clunk-clunk of weighing scales
bok choy tofu carrots ginger cilantro
all for under five

on to the food stalls:
order chwee kueh and
hot tofu pudding

settle down at one of the communal stone tables
eavesdrop on Singlish
ever-present din and hot pulse
of lively strangers

I feel an ache for lost years with each bitter sip
of kopi-o from the old-fashioned ceramic cup

crackled surface beneath
the bluish green flowery motif
sad yet beautiful

when I was 13, I wrote an essay for class
Members of my Family
         described my father stout as a teapot
         my mother's eyes dark and gleaming
         as the kopi she drank

deep inside her aging brain
that spark still lives
         moments when her spirit rouses
         if there's a tiger in front of me
         I could slay it

         once again I
         cross time zones and meanings
         back to my life in Vancouver

         accustomed to
         taking this journey alone

my mother has consistently refused
to leave her familiar life—
how natural, easy to understand

each of us entrenched
in our attachments

I walk down Main
through Chinatown
sensing disappearances and lingering shadows

women of the Downtown Eastside
the poor and elderly in SROs in Chinatown

familiar faces
could you spare some change?
in front of New Town bakery

businesses closing down:
herbal medicine shops
restaurants
bakeries
the framing shop torched by Stanley Cup rioters

even Hello Kitty has it rough on East Pender

the concept called
Vancouver turns 125

post-Pickton, post 2010
signs of so-called revival
constant looming threat of skyscrapers
new pubs, eateries, clothing stores
all owned by non-Chinese

challenge my romance about Chinatowns
as enclaves

longing to be visible
to distinguish ourselves from others
complex tapestry of cultural practices

a distinct difference between
differentiation and segregation

I love coming here
rekindling memories of growing up
as granddaughter of a Chinese physician
in Singapore

names of herbs and medicinal concoctions
now interest me

I look for things I failed to discover in my childhood
        cordyceps, fu ling, dong quai
            white cloud's ears, wong lo kat...
each time I look, something new

৬—

Old man in the opposite booth mirrors my future with his
seasoned jowls, his weary eyes disinterested in youth's foolish
indulgences. Affirms that I too am travelling away from birth,
settling into my private autumn. I feel the buzz of Filipino
families in the warm ambience of New Town bakery—their
bright voices chirp at the edge of my attention.

We could almost forget, sitting here, that we are forever
foreign in this adopted country.

Dianne the waitress still wears her hair in a voluminous
roll-up bun, now dyed jet black—looks like she recently
stepped out from the Tang dynasty court, voluptuous and
swaggering all at once, a cowboy courtesan in the
21st century.

৬—

travelling with others
on buses and Skytrains where
faces wearing public cool
contrast with those unable to conceal
their afflictions

          curious about others
          wonder if they wonder too

rhythms of privacy
in a boundless sphere

           mask vulnerabilities with earphones
           finger auto-swipes left to right

tap tap tap
of virtual life
simulated activity
speeded stimulation

atmospheres
rife with tremulous exchange—
frenetic acquisition of
friendships on Facebook
bursts of Twitter

rote circuitry reflex
lessening the window for gasping
for wondering or doubt

digital time unitary
                  overshadows analog nuance

less uncertainty, it appears
no room for error, it seems

do our minds habituate?
                  as if life never changes
                  as if death couldn't possibly happen
                  this very moment
                  come unannounced

and yet—

old men and women at the front of the bus
smile whimsically at babies in strollers
Muslim man delights in
his rambunctious teenaged daughter
at the back of the bus
young Taiwanese women discuss university
near the doors

woken up from sleep's stupor
by a poem's whisper

I caress
soft skin of keys
striking contrast to
the planet loud
with catastrophe

earthquake upon earthquake in northeast Japan
tsunamis
nuclear leakages

massive starvation in Somalia
suicide bombings in Afghanistan
double shooting in Norway
        18-year-old Bano Rashid shot dead on Utoya Island
        had fled Iraq with her family
        to seek refuge in Norway

endless, continuous onslaught of trauma

the ache
a long sinuous wave
reaching us on this shore

and we, pained by helpless grief
a strange brand of distanced suffering

shaken toward
denial or an opening

mono no aware
sensitivity toward other beings

Kali Yuga times
when the bull of morality
shadowed by the dark age
is left with only one leg to stand on

losing the base of invincibility
losing the balance that once was

a deep well of grief
pools over my heart

one day one day one day
another generation
may transcend fear's paranoid grasp

to answer hatred with love

in dreams we've been separated
missing each other
unable to stay close

my mother, once the ground of my being
until I sought meaning elsewhere

the urgencies of others
cleaved us
the needs of others
join us

I listen to her voice over the telephone
a weave of
vigour and vulnerability
her moments of happiness
like rare nectar for my spirit

we were alienated
yet driven as if by some cellular hunger
toward making peace

as if she and I
were cast into Indra's Net
along with all other mothers and daughters

tossing innuendo
entangling intention
livid and loved
in the gasp and pause

bent cedar branch above
this familiar route home
weighted with the history
of countless travellers

sound of earth's groaning

crunch of boots
on gravel a textured
detour from

roar of traffic on Main
car demons
fast fleeing
in the dusk

damp cold air presses against my skin
enabling constraint

a stranger's shadow
down the narrow alley
no, not near there—

in this world rife with such tragedy
what could I offer?

simply this wish to reconcile
without pretence

indigo electric pink pulses float off other skins

twilight zones
reptilian codes
energy folds

bodies skin hands
the slightest movement
the way breath is stifled
or released

phantom, adj.   hand, n.

     illusive   *a worker*
     spectral   *influence*

phantom, n.   hand, v.t.

     a deceitful appearance   *manipulate*
     an immaterial form   *transfer*

in solitude

I raise my hands up
then let them descend
back into my lap
left palm over right

bring down peace

> who is this ego?
> where is the self?

A bruise? Or the shadow of a bruise? Memory of my first
dream, a room where I had yearned to reach another.
Wishing in metaphors. From the centre of my chest, an
illusion cracks open. The truth surfaces, a need to feel the
pulse of my own life.

*The ceiling turns from red to midnight. When it fades to
grey I am standing in a corridor, uncertain of where I am,
this slim fragment of an unknown house. No windows, yet
bars of light stream across the walls on either side as if
urging me on.*

*I reach out to feel the light. Trace with my fingers as if
decoding a secret.*

moving out toward the world
surely not a simple case of jettison
from refuge to chaos

in a gasp for living
the breath a blade
slicing through

Notes

epigraph

Quote from *The Cbap*. Phnom Penh: Reyum Publishing, Khmer Literature Collection, undated.

Quote, André Breton, http://www.brainyquote.com/quotes/authors/a/andre_breton.html

wandering phantom

The quote on page 6, *if there's nothing else you remember/remember this: it all depends,* was uttered frequently by my Psychology 100 professor Barney Gilmore throughout that first year at U of T. Hannah Arendt was a German-Jewish political theorist who coined the term "banality of evil" in her book *Eichmann in Jerusalem* (Penguin Classics, 1963), in which she posits that evil actions are the result of individuals' thoughtless obedience to authorities. Maria Torok and Nicolas Abraham were Hungarians whose lives were disrupted by the Holocaust. They posited that the traumatic power of an event depended on the person's intrapsychic experience. Their work sought to radicalize psychoanalytic thinking, resisting doctrinaire tendencies in the theory and practice of psychoanalysis (see Maria Yassa's 2002 article on their work in the *Scandinavian Psychoanalytic Review*).

In this section as well as throughout other sections of the book, I've made allusions to *phantom* as the ejection of a hidden kernel, contrasting kernel with the outer shell of existence; while these notions are based on Torok and Abraham's ideas, I've taken poetic liberties with my interpretations of these ideas. Torok and Abraham spoke about traumatic elements in experiences that became impossible to integrate and hence were dissociated from the conscious self. They referred to the traumatic "foreign entity" as a *psychic phantom*. I am not sure to what extent they were aware of Pierre Janet's work in the late 1800s and early 1900s on traumatic memories and dissociation—their ideas share a great deal of resonance with Janet's.

The book alluded to on page 12 is Roland Barthes' *A Lover's Discourse* published by Hill and Wang, 1979; and the quote (*raised arms of Desire… wide-open arms of Need*) is found on page 16 of that book.

Mention of René Magritte on page 19 refers to his 1953 painting *Golconda*, where men in bowler hats are floating in the sky.

On page 21, *Christ the magic saviour…* was actually a street person's lyrics sung to the song "Puff the Magic Dragon" by Peter, Paul and Mary (1963).

unspoken

The excerpt at the top of page 25 is a translation of Pierre Janet's patient Irène's response to being questioned about her recollections of her mother's passing; on the same page, *open your mouth, drink, answer me* were phrases that Irène used to address her mother's corpse. This material is found in an essay by Bessel van der Kolk and Onno van der Hart, "The Intrusive Past: The flexibility of memory and the Engraving of Trauma," in *Trauma: Explorations in Memory* (Baltimore: The Johns Hopkins University Press, 1995). Pierre Janet was a psychiatrist who observed and described traumatic symptoms in his patients. He was a contemporary of Sigmund Freud's; Janet's work with patients at the Salpêtrière significantly informed 20th-century thinking about post-traumatic stress disorder. At the bottom of page 25: *Ergriffenheit* is the term Carl Jung used in his 1936 essay on Wotan, to describe the state of being seized or possessed (in *Collected Works*, Volume 10; Routledge and Kegan Paul, London, 1970).

It is only for convenience that we speak of it as… (page 26). Translation of Pierre Janet's idea found in above-mentioned essay by Bessel van der Kolk and Onno van der Hart. The change of male to female pronoun in the quote is mine.

Page 32: a mala is a set of beads strung together for the specific purpose of keeping count while reciting mantras or chanting.

...*a history that literally has no place*... (page 34) taken from Cathy Carruth's "Recapturing the Past: Introduction," in *Trauma: Explorations in Memory* (Baltimore: The Johns Hopkins University Press, 1995), page 153.

sojourn

The various temples mentioned in this section were: Todaiji in Nara, Horyuji just south of Nara, Sanjusangendo in Kyoto. Deer roam the Nara koen (park) outside Todaiji.

On page 41, kembutsu-nin means sightseer.

I was starting to work on my novel *The Walking Boy* at that time, and curious about the remnants of Tang dynasty influences which remained in evidence in Nara's temples. A great deal of Buddhist art and architecture had been destroyed in Chang'an, the Western capital during the Tang dynasty in China.

Daibutsu is the enormous Buddha statue in the main hall of Todaiji, hence the hall's name is Daibutsuden (page 42).

page 43: kohii, Japanese coffee

page 44:

unagi, freshwater eel

tsukemono, pickles

gohan, steamed white rice

noren, traditional Japanese fabric dividers hung at entrances to shops, or between rooms, in doorways or at windows

page 45: Yumechigai-Kannon means Avalokiteshvara for good dreams

page 46: *bus 205... stop at...* from *Lonely Planet Guide* (2nd edition, 2001); a ryokan is a traditional Japanese inn or guesthouse

page 47: tatami flooring is usually made of rice straw

oden, a miso-based stew with various ingredients, often eaten in the winter

sento, a public bath, segregated by gender

On page 49, there are various references to food. Bonito flakes result from a complex process of preparing the bonito fish by cooking, then having it wood-smoked, put through fermentation and further sun-dried before being thinly shaved into their final form as flakes to be used either as garnish or as an important ingredient in a broth base called dashi. Umeboshi are pickled ume plums.

Also on page 49: geisha are women who are professional entertainers, skilled as hostesses, and in singing, dancing and playing musical instruments; maiko are apprentices preparing to become geisha.

On page 50, I make reference to Haruki Murakami's novel *The Wind-Up Bird Chronicle*. It was groundbreaking in many regards, including exposing the cruelty of Japanese military during their invasion of Manchuria. There is a horrific account of the flaying/skinning of a human in that novel.

The quote at the top of page 51, *The pleasure that comes from pleasurable surroundings...* is taken from *Master of the Three Ways: Reflections of a Chinese Sage on Living a Satisfying Life,* by Hung Ying-ming, translated by William Scott Wilson, English Translation © 2009 by William Scott Wilson.

Also on page 51: Nobuyoshi Araki's exhibit *Hana Jinsei* was showing at the Kyoto Museum of Contemporary Art while I was there in December 2002.

Page 52: Jomon period lasted from about 14,000 BC to about 300 BC, when Japan was inhabited by a hunter-gatherer culture.

Kannon (page 53) is the Japanese name for Avalokiteshvara (Sanskrit name) or Quanyin (Chinese).

On page 54, I pose a question about the ground of our being. Paul Tillich was a German philosopher who coined the notion of God as the ground of our being. This Christian theological position is radically different than one that views God as a separate being.

sinuous

This section focuses on my experiences practising ki aikido. Ki aikido is one of the schools of aikido, the art of peace developed by Morehei Ueshiba.

The principles of ki aikido listed on page 58 are set out according to the Ki Federation of Great Britain (www.kifederationofgreatbritain.co.uk), the umbrella organization to which the Canadian Ki Federation belongs.

On page 61: kami is the Japanese word for divine being or Spirit, particularly in the Shinto religion; jo is a wooden staff about fifty inches long.

On page 64, the Morehei Ueshiba quote is taken from *The Art of Peace,* translations by John Stevens (Boston: Shambhala, 2007).

On page 66, *counting weapons is like counting votes* found at www.Guardian.co.uk (September 2009, Julian Berger)

At the top of page 68, *The mind of attachment... from The Unfettered Mind* by Takuan Soho, translated by William Scott Wilson, English Translation ©1986 and 2002 by William Scott Wilson.

True Victory is Self-Victory on page 72, taken from *The Art of Peace.*

base

There are 3 newspaper headlines on page 77 which were taken from the web. These refer to 3 boats of Fujian migrants who arrived off the shores of Vancouver Island in July 1999.

On page 78: Song by the female Fujian boat migrants is taken from *Movement Across Borders: Chinese Women Migrants in China.* Report by Direct Action Against Refugee Exploitation, April 2001, page 5.

The reference on page 79 to "Orient" being a fenced-in stage is based on Edward Said's comment in *Orientalism* (UK:Vintage Books, 1978, page 63).

On page 81, *The visions of men are widened by travel...* quote by

Gurdit Singh Sandhu found online: http://en.wikipedia.org/wiki/Komagata_Maru_incident

He was an Indo-Canadian immigration pioneer in Singapore who chartered the *Komagata Maru* to carry Punjabi migrants from India to Canada.

The quote on page 82 about pseudologia phantastica is taken from Carl Jung's essay, "After the Catastrophe" in *Civilization in Transition*, volume 10, pages 203-204, *The Collected Works of C.G. Jung* (Princeton: Bollingen Series, 1945)

Definition on page 83 of *Ergreifer—one who seizes*—also taken from Jung's essay.

On pages 89-90, I make references to various foods and food-sellers. In many parts of Asia, there still exist wet markets—where fresh vegetables and meats are sold, without the use of refrigeration; chwee kueh are steamed rice cakes topped with fried preserved radish bits; kopi is the Malay word for coffee, and kopi-o is the slang term for black coffee without sugar or milk.

On page 92, I have a list of Chinese herbs: cordyceps, fu ling, dong quai…and a famous brew called wong lo kat.

Reference on page 96: Kali Yuga is the Hindu term for Dark Age, when all religions are on the wane. It is the last stage the world goes through, according to Indian Scriptures. Kali Yuga is associated with the apocalyptic demon Kali.

At the bottom of page 96: *to answer hatred with love,* quote from Norwegian Prime Minister's pledge at funeral of Breivik's victims (http://www.independent.co.uk/news/world/europe/we-will-answer-hatred-with-love-and-honour-our-heroes-2328666.html)

Indra's Net (page 97) is a metaphor that refers to the interconnection and interdependency among all beings and phenomena.

Acknowledgements

I wish to acknowledge permissions granted for quotes from the following:

The Cbap. Phnom Penh: Reyum Publishing, Khmer Literature Collection, undated.

Caruth, Cathy, ed., *Trauma: Explorations in Memory*. pp. 153, 160, 161. © 1995 The Johns Hopkins University Press. Reprinted with permission of The Johns Hopkins University Press.

From *Master of the Three Ways: Reflections of a Chinese Sage on Living a Satisfying Life*, by Hung Ying-ming, translated by William Scott Wilson, English Translation (c) 2009 by William Scott Wilson. Reprinted by arrangement with Shambhala Publications Inc., Boston, MA. www.shambhala.com.

From *The Art of Peace*, translations by John Stevens (Boston: Shambhala, 2007).

From *The Unfettered Mind*, by Takuan Soho, translated by William Scott Wilson, English Translation ©1986 and 2002 by William Scott Wilson. Reprinted by arrangement with Shambhala Publications Inc., Boston, MA. www.shambhala.com.

The Collected Works of C.G. Jung, Vol. 10: Civilization in Transition by C.G. Jung. Copyright, Princeton University Press, 1945.

This book would not have been possible without the expertise and care of many. In particular, I wish to thank Clarise Forster, editor; and the folks at Turnstone Press.

I am grateful to Rita Wong and Cathy Stonehouse, who provided critical feedback at the late stages, and contributed significantly toward developing the narrative framework.

Years ago, Dayaneetha De Silva gave me the precious gift of a booklet called *The Cbap*, published by a Khmer company called Reyum in Phnom Penh. I use a quote from this booklet in the epigraph; the idea for the title of this book derives from that quote.

Lisa Robertson reminded me of the psychoanalytic work of Torok and Abraham, and inspired me to elaborate on the notion of phantom and kernel.

Thanks to those who read earlier versions or portions of this manuscript over the years and offered encouraging comments: Carmen Rodriguez, Nancy Richler, Daphne Marlatt, Kevin Spetifore, Wayne Nagata and Kesia Nagata.

Thanks also to Hideaki Kanamaru, who provided the author photograph and took video clips of me reading excerpts from the book.

Excerpts from earlier versions of this book appeared in the following anthologies: *Swallowing Clouds* (Arsenal Pulp, 2002) and *Open Field* (Persea, 2005); also, in the following magazines: *West Coast Line*, no. 43, Spring 2004, *West Coast Line*, no. 71, Fall 2011, *Poetry Is Dead—Queer Issue,* Summer/Autumn 2012.

Last but not least, my profound appreciation goes out to the many individuals who had suffered heinous acts of violence and were brave enough to share their innermost experiences with me. They remain unnamed to preserve their privacy and right to confidentiality.